MW00980059

SEVEN WONDERS OF THE WORLD

SEVEN WONDERS OF THE ANCIENT WORLD

A MyReportLinks.com Book

Michelle Laliberte

MyReportLinks.com Books

an imprint of

Enslow Publishers, Inc.

Box 398, 40 Industrial Road
Berkeley Heights, NJ 07922
USA

MyReportLinks.com Books, an imprint of Enslow Publishers, Inc. MyReportLinks® is a registered trademark of Enslow Publishers, Inc.

Library of Congress Cataloging-in-Publication Data

Laliberte, Michelle.
Seven wonders of the ancient world / Michelle Laliberte.
p. cm. — (Seven wonders of the world)
Includes bibliographical references and index.
ISBN 0-7660-5293-1
1. Seven Wonders of the World—Juvenile literature. I. Title. II. Series.
N5333.L35 2005
722—dc22
2004026458

Printed in the United States of America

10 9 8 7 6 5 4 3 2 1

To Our Readers:
Through the purchase of this book, you and your library gain access to the Report Links that specifically back up this book.
The Publisher will provide access to the Report Links that back up this book and will keep these Report Links up to date on **www.myreportlinks.com** for five years from the book's first publication date.
We have done our best to make sure all Internet addresses in this book were active and appropriate when we went to press. However, the author and the Publisher have no control over, and assume no liability for, the material available on those Internet sites or on other Web sites they may link to.
The usage of the MyReportLinks.com Books Web site is subject to the terms and conditions stated on the Usage Policy Statement on **www.myreportlinks.com**.
A password may be required to access the Report Links that back up this book. The password is found on the bottom of page 4 of this book.
Any comments or suggestions can be sent by e-mail to comments@myreportlinks.com or to the address on the back cover.

Photo Credits: © Alaa K. Ashmawy, p. 9; © 1997 Cable News Network, p. 8; © 2000 The British Museum, p. 31; © Corel Corporation, pp. 1, 26; © James Grout, pp. 22, 28; © Lee Krystek, 1998, pp. 19, 24, 37; © UNESCO, p. 41; E. Scalzo, p. 32; Enslow Publishers, Inc., p. 6; Hemera Image Express, p. 14; Howard David Johnson, pp. 10, 17, 21, 25, 30, 34, 38; Keith Hobbs/*Saudi Aramco World*/PADIA, p. 39; Michael Grimsdale/*Saudi Aramco World*/PADIA, p. 3; MyReportLinks.com Books, p. 4; National Geographic Society, p. 12; Photos.com, p. 35.

Cover Photo: © Corel Corporation

Cover Description: The Pyramids of Giza.

Chapter Opener Illustrations by Howard David Johnson.

Contents

MyReportLinks.com Books

Great Books, Great Links, Great for Research!

The Internet sites featured in this book can save you hours of research time. These Internet sites—we call them **"Report Links"**—are constantly changing, but we keep them up to date on our Web site.

When you see this "Approved Web Site" logo, you will know that we are directing you to a great Internet site that will help you with your research.

Give it a try! Type http://www.myreportlinks.com into your browser, click on the series title and enter the password, then click on the book title, and scroll down to the Report Links listed for this book.

The Report Links will bring you to great source documents, photographs, and illustrations. MyReportLinks.com Books save you time, feature Report Links that are kept up to date, and make report writing easier than ever! A complete listing of the Report Links can be found on pages 42–43 at the back of the book.

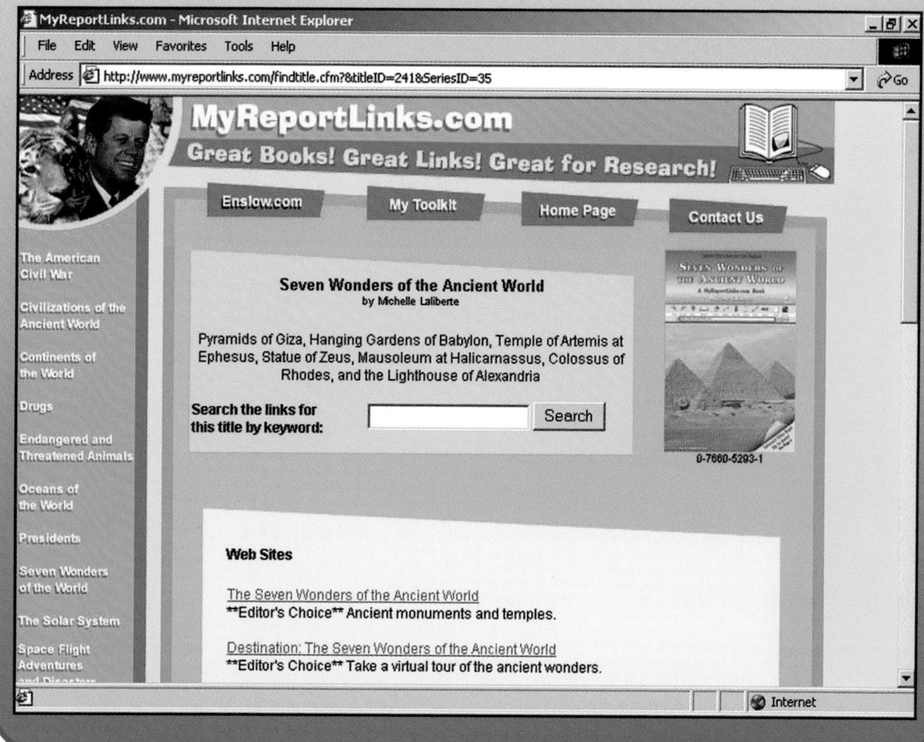

Please see "To Our Readers" on the copyright page for important information about this book, the MyReportLinks.com Web site, and the Report Links that back up this book.

Please enter **SWA1043** if asked for a password.

Seven Wonders of the Ancient World Facts

Pyramids of Giza

- Located in Giza, Egypt, along the west bank of the Nile River.
- The pyramids are the oldest and only surviving ancient wonder.
- The Pyramids of Giza were built somewhere between 2700 and 2500 B.C.

Hanging Gardens of Babylon

- The gardens are thought to have been located in Babylon, near present-day Baghdad, Iraq.
- Babylonian king Nebuchadnezzar is credited with having the gardens built.
- It is likely that they were built between 605 and 562 B.C.

Temple of Artemis at Ephesus

- The Temple of Artemis at Ephesus was built in what is now southwestern Turkey.
- It is one of the largest temples built by ancient Greek sculptors.
- The temple is often referred to as The Temple of Diana, the Roman name for the goddess Artemis.

Statue of Zeus

- The remains of the temple that housed the Statue of Zeus have been found in the ancient Greek city of Olympia.
- The statue was built in honor of the Olympic Games.
- It is estimated that the Statue of Zeus was built around 450 B.C.

Mausoleum at Halicarnassus

- Built about 353 B.C. by Queen Artemisia to honor her husband, King Mausolus.
- Due to the size of Mausolus' burial site, the word *mausoleum* came to mean a large tomb.
- The Mausoleum of Halicarnassus was located in what is now Bodrum,Turkey.

Colossus of Rhodes

- Located on the island of Rhodes, the colossus is said to have watched over the harbor.
- The large bronze statue was a representation of the sun god, Helios, also known as Apollo.
- Built around 282 B.C., it took the sculptor, Chares, twelve years to complete.

The Lighthouse (Pharos) of Alexandria

- Located on the island of Pharos, off the coast of Alexandria, Egypt.
- The Lighthouse of Alexandria is believed to be the first and tallest lighthouse ever constructed.
- The lighthouse was likely built about 280 B.C., and stood until the A.D. 1200s.

Chapter 1 ▶

SEVEN WONDERS OF THE ANCIENT WORLD

Throughout history, the seven wonders of the ancient world have dazzled people with their beauty, size, and sheer magnificence. Majestic pyramids, grand monuments, and towering statues are among the many wonders to have graced the list. The wonders have evoked strong emotions. They also have awakened a curiosity in those who are astounded at the mystery of how such wonders were constructed without the use of modern machines or tools. To make things even more interesting and debatable,

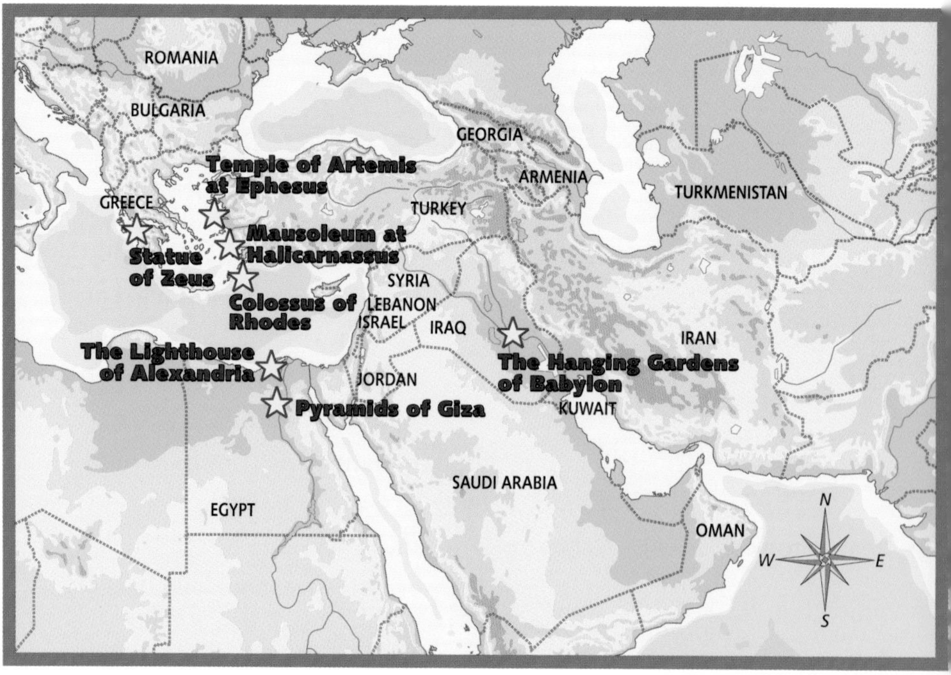

This is a modern map of Europe and the Middle East showing where the seven wonders of the ancient world would be located today. The Pyramids of Giza are the only ancient wonder still standing.

there is only one surviving wonder left in today's world. Much of what we know about most of the ancient wonders comes from texts left behind by ancient historians or from images on old coins.

The Seven Wonders of the Ancient World

Most experts agree that the seven wonders of the ancient world are the Pyramids of Giza, the Hanging Gardens of Babylon, the Temple of Artemis, the Statue of Zeus, the Mausoleum at Halicarnassus, the Colossus of Rhodes, and the Lighthouse (Pharos) of Alexandria. Five of the seven wonders were carved, cast, constructed, or sculpted by the best Greek artists and architects. Each wonder exhibits the representation of early human achievement through the advanced technological skill of those who built it, but each does so in an entirely different way.

The Pyramids of Giza are the only remaining wonder of the seven that still exists close to its original form. They represent a supreme example of stone building. Their mass amazes all who are lucky enough to visit them.

The Hanging Gardens of Babylon are thought to have been designed as a present from a king to his homesick wife. The gardens were supposedly laid out on a brick terrace 394 square feet (120 meters squared) in area and 82 feet (25 meters) high.[1] They had massive gardens, trees, and bushes that decorated the tall sloping terraces. Water was brought in by means of a chain pump that pulled the water from the nearby Euphrates River. The water would flow down the terraces, spreading out to all the gardens. The gardens were an example of skill in harnessing running water.

The Temple of Artemis at Ephesus was a massive monument that took more than 120 years to build. It was one of the largest temples built in ancient times. Its enormous size alone allows the temple to capture a place on the list of seven wonders.

The Statue of Zeus was an ivory and gold statue of the god Zeus. It was made by the Greek sculptor Phidias in the Greek city of Olympia, where the first Olympic Games took place.

The Mausoleum at Halicarnassus was a large tomb built to hold the remains of Mausolus, ruler of Caria, and his wife, Queen Artemisia. Built in 353 B.C., this 148-foot- (45-meter-) high marble tomb is the reason all large tombs since then have been called mausoleums. Today, the area once called Caria is located in southwest Turkey.

The Colossus of Rhodes looked like an ancient-day Statue of Liberty. It was located by the harbor of the Mediterranean island of Rhodes in what is now Greece. The statue was thought to have stood guard against incoming enemy ships. Built around 282 B.C., this 120-foot (33-meter) colossal statue dedicated to the sun god, Helios, demonstrated exceptional skill in bronze casting.

The seventh wonder, the Lighthouse of Alexandria, the tallest building in the ancient world, took fifteen years to build and stood 443 feet (135 meters) high. It is believed to have been more like a tower than a lighthouse. Built in three separate levels, the

Destinations: The Seven Wonders of the Ancient World

This CNN site provides a brief background on the seven wonders of the ancient world. A map marking the location of each wonder is also included.

EDITOR'S CHOICE

Access this Web site from http://www.myreportlinks.com

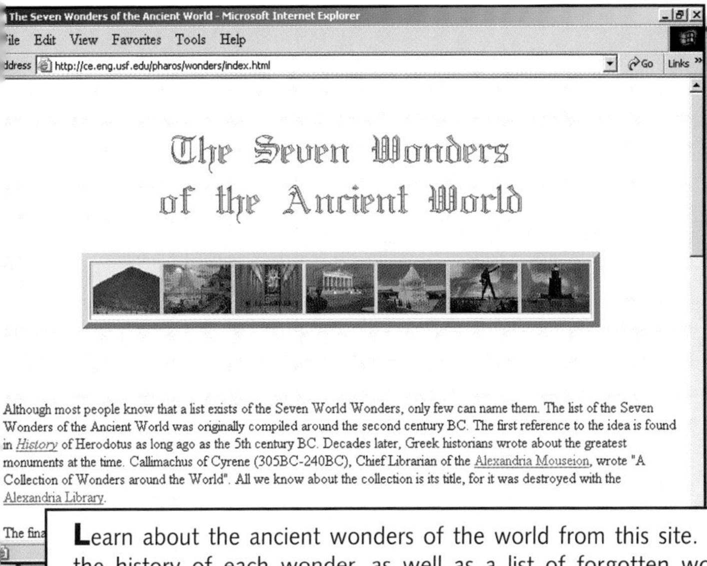

The Seven Wonders of the Ancient World

Learn about the ancient wonders of the world from this site. Information about the history of each wonder, as well as a list of forgotten wonders and a map are included.

EDITOR'S CHOICE

Access this Web site from http://www.myreportlinks.com

lighthouse did not resemble a modern-day lighthouse. It was a rectangular-shaped tower. There was a mirror on top to reflect sunlight during the day, and a fire would guide ships safely into port at night.

Despite the differences in the designs and styles of each of the seven wonders, they all provide proof of the advanced capabilities of ancient technologies.

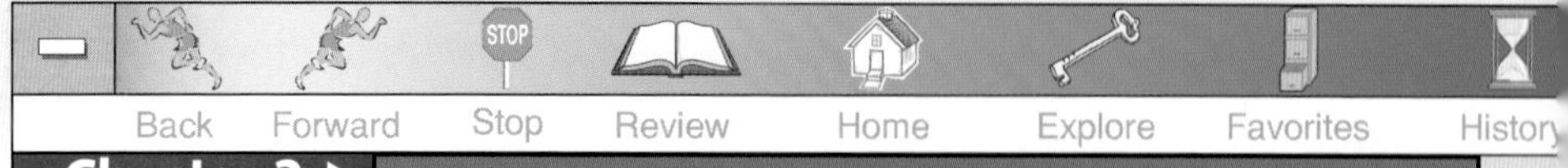

Chapter 2 ▶

Pyramids of Giza

The only one of the seven wonders of the ancient world still in existence are the Pyramids of Giza. The sheer size of the pyramids, built from 2700 to 2500 B.C., still astonishes visitors to this day. Located in Giza, Egypt, on the west bank of the Nile River near Cairo, the Giza pyramids are the oldest and best preserved surviving member of the ancient wonders. However, a mystery still exists over how the ancient builders were able to erect such amazing structures at a time before modern tools or technologies existed. There is also some debate among scholars whether only Khufu, the largest of the three pyramids, should be considered a wonder of the ancient world.

Historians and archaeologists estimate that the Pyramids of Giza were built between 2700 and 2500 B.C.

Meaning of the Pyramids and Preparation of the Site

The pyramid of King Khufu is also known as the Great Pyramid. For more than four thousand years, it was the tallest human-made structure in the world.[1] The other two pyramids are named for King Khafre and King Menkaure.

The Egyptian pyramids are gigantic structures that house royal tombs. They were designed to be massive, bulky, and solid. This was done to protect the king's body and keep all his treasures buried with him safe from grave robbers and thieves. Many believe that the pyramid was shaped the way it is to serve as a ramp to the sky. The ramp was intended to assist the king in his ascent to heaven. The angle of each side of the pyramid measured exactly 51 degrees, 51 minutes.

Great care was taken in choosing an appropriate construction site for the pyramids. The ancient Egyptians selected the Giza plateau. This spot was probably picked for its dominating position above the Nile Valley's west bank. Egyptians associated the west with the setting sun and death. The limestone ridge also provided a solid foundation for the massive weight of the pyramids, as well as ample material for building their solid cores.

Building the Pyramids

Once the site was chosen, the area had to be laid out and leveled off to provide a good foundation. Egyptians used their knowledge of the stars to help them line up the pyramid foundations very accurately to face the north, south, east, and west. They usually achieved this with an error of less than half a degree.[2] It took more than ten thousand laborers almost twenty years to build Khufu. Rising about 450 feet (137 meters) and covering 13 acres (5.26 hectares), the Great Pyramid is an impressive sight to behold.[3] When it was built, Khufu was even taller than it is today. Over

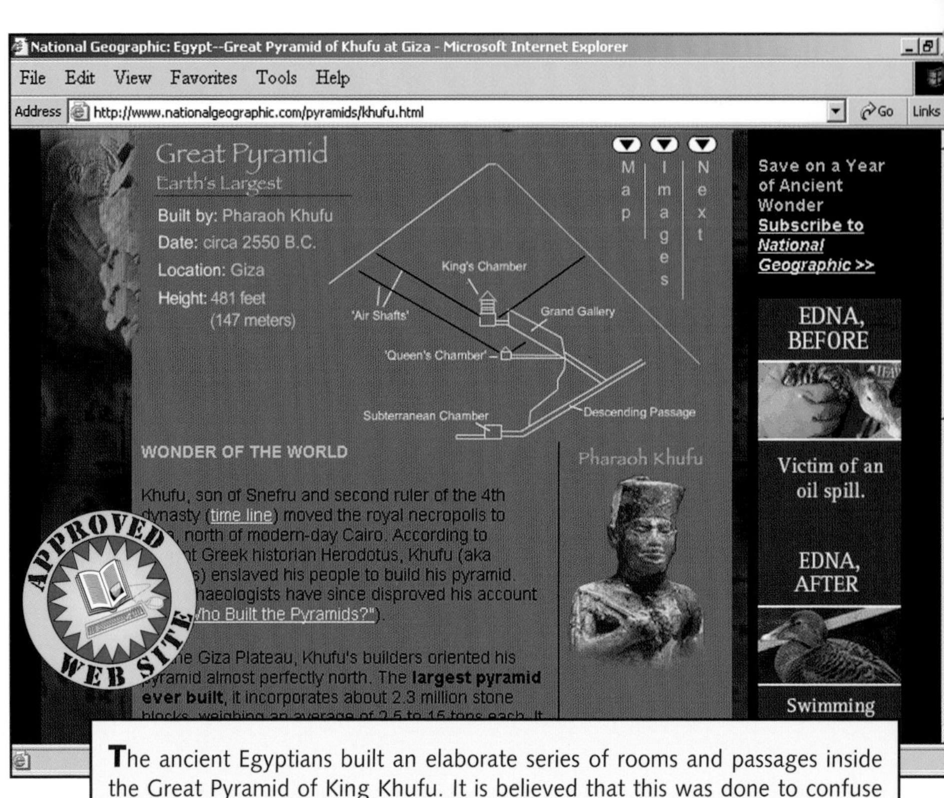

The ancient Egyptians built an elaborate series of rooms and passages inside the Great Pyramid of King Khufu. It is believed that this was done to confuse burglars. This sketch can be found on *National Geographic*'s Web site called **Egypt: Secrets of the Ancient World.**

thousands of years, approximately thirty feet (9.14 meters) of stone has eroded off the top.

The blocks used for the core of the pyramids were dug up from just south of the pyramid. The Egyptians excavated and transported the blocks by leveling the area. They carved a grid of shallow trenches into the bedrock. They would then flood the trenches with water to flatten the area to the level they wanted.[4] The limestone blocks used in the pyramids weighed an average of 2.5 tons (2.54 metric tons). As laborers built the pyramids higher, they used lighter and lighter blocks. So, the blocks used for the top of the pyramid were easier to carry.[5] The number of laborers dragging a block would be determined by its weight.

The pyramids were built by farm laborers—not slaves as originally believed. They worked on the pyramids when the Nile flooded their fields and they were unable to farm.

How Were the Blocks Lifted?

One of the most difficult things to figure out about how the pyramids were built was the method used to lift the blocks onto the pyramid. Scholars want to know how the Egyptians lifted those heavy limestone blocks with such simple and primitive tools as were available at the time.

Most archaeologists think laborers used a series of winding ramps to drag the millions of blocks into their final resting places on the pyramids. These ramps looked somewhat like a ramp that people use today to drive up and down parking decks. No such ramps, however, have ever been found at Giza. But ramps have been found at the sites of other pyramids built during a similar era. These findings suggest at least five different systems of ramps were used around the time period that the Pyramids of Giza were built.[6]

It seems likely that other ways of raising blocks might have been used as the pyramid construction progressed. Most of a pyramid's mass is in the bottom two thirds. The Egyptians would have to use a series of small ramps to keep the heavy building blocks moving toward the section they were working on.[7] When they got close to the top, the blocks would be moved up the ramps much more slowly. The workers needed to go slow to make sure the blocks were positioned properly.

Each block was cut to shape only after it had been moved to its final position to ensure an exact fit with the blocks on either side of it. The casing blocks of the Great Pyramid are so tightly positioned next to one another that it is often impossible to slide a knife blade between them.[8] A substance called gypsum mortar was used to fill any gaps and may also have been used as a lubricant to ease the positioning of the blocks.

Internal Layout of the Pyramids

The Great Pyramid is unique because it has a very complex design of rooms and passageways. The rooms are surrounded by a wall of fine Turah limestone. Built to withstand enormous pressure, the King's Chamber was made entirely of pink granite.[9] Above it are five smaller rooms roofed with huge granite beams. This design would deflect the weight of the pyramid away from the ceiling of the burial chamber. Narrow shafts in the Grand Gallery, approximately 3.1 square inches (twenty centimeters square), lead to the King's Chamber from two upper chambers. They are aligned toward the constellation Orion and the circumpolar stars so that the dead king's soul could travel to these stars.[10]

This is a photo of the pyramid of King Khafre. You can see that the top of this pyramid still has some of its original limestone casing.

The inner chambers of Khafre's and Menkaure's pyramids are below ground level and were excavated from bedrock. Khafre's pyramid has two simple rooms. Menkaure's pyramid is smaller, but it has a more complex layout of rooms and passageways. One of the rooms is even decorated.

What Remains of the Pyramids Today

The Giza pyramids remain mostly intact except for the tunnels dug by robbers. The only major difference today is that almost all of the white limestone casing is gone. The casing was put over the outside of the stone building blocks to protect them from weather damage. In the Middle Ages, the pyramids were stripped of their limestone, which was used for building and construction work in Cairo. It was much easier to strip the casing blocks from the pyramids than to unearth new building material. Only a tiny section of the casing remains at the tip of Khafre's pyramid. Still, it provides a small glimpse of the limestone's original appearance.

The exploration and mapping of the Giza plateau has been going on since the 1600s and is still in progress. Careful collaboration and research between Egyptologists and other specialists, such as engineers, geologists, and astronomers, can help provide insight and details surrounding the mystery of the pyramids and the ancient people who built these magnificent monuments.

Chapter 3

The Hanging Gardens of Babylon

The Hanging Gardens of Babylon were built from about 605 to 562 B.C. by King Nebuchadnezzar II. He was the son of King Nabopolassar, a famous king in the history of the Babylonian Empire. Babylon, an ancient city in Mesopotamia, was located near modern-day Baghdad, Iraq. The Hanging Gardens of Babylon made the list of the seven wonders of the ancient world because they represent the majesty of the Babylonian culture and the advanced architecture of its people.

Description of the Gardens

There have been many opinions throughout history about what the Hanging Gardens of Babylon actually looked like. There are even many who doubt whether the gardens actually existed. There is no remaining evidence still standing.

The most likely story is that King Nebuchadnezzar II built the Hanging Gardens for his homesick wife, Amyitis. Amyitis thought Mesopotamia's flat, dry environment was depressing. She was from Media, a green and mountainous land in what is now the country of Iran. In a gesture to show his love, Nebuchadnezzar decided to build her an artificial mountain with rooftop gardens. These gardens were a man-made paradise in the middle of a desert.

In this harsh and barren environment, Nebuchadnezzar succeeded in building Amyitis a lavish rooftop garden. He made the gardens resemble a natural wilderness in Media, with rolling hills covered with lots of different kinds of trees and flowers. The gardens sloped downward to look like a hillside. This was meant to

This painting of the Hanging Gardens of Babylon shows a woman, possibly Queen Amyitis, enjoying the gardens that Nebuchadnezzar had built for her. Many scholars debate whether the Hanging Gardens even existed.

satisfy Amyitis' desire for a mountainous area. Terraces with beds of many exotic flowers were built into the hill. The gardens also had plants that were cultivated and thrived in a man-made above-ground environment.

Nebuchadnezzar had trees, such as cedar, almond, ebony, olive, and oak, sent to Babylon. Branches dangled over the heads of those who walked along the terraces. Brilliantly colored flowers and grapevines decorated everything. Stone columns and cube-shaped pillars supported the lavish flower terraces. The pillars were hollow and filled with soil to grow large trees.[1] There were four tiers of archways that helped keep the area cool. The fountains that flowed down the tops of the four tiers provided a refreshing mist. Areas of shade from the planted trees created a lush and magical environment.

The entire structure covered an area of 394 feet (120 meters) square and was about 82 feet (25 meters) high. The gardens were as tall as the city walls of Babylon, which according to historian Herodotus, were reported to be 320 feet (97.6 meters) high.[2] A basement with fourteen large rooms and underground crypts were also part of the garden.

Use of Hydro-Engineering in the Hanging Gardens

The Greek geographer Strabo described the gardens in the first century B.C. He wrote: "The ascent to the highest story is by stairs, and at their side are water engines, by means of which persons, appointed expressly for the purpose, are continually employed raising water from the Euphrates into the garden."[3]

Strabo pointed out what was probably the most astonishing part of the garden. Because Babylon rarely received enough rain to maintain the water of the gardens, they were irrigated using water from the nearby Euphrates River. This meant lifting the water high into the air so it could trickle down through the terraces at each level. No one is quite sure how this was achieved, but it was most likely done using a chain pump.[4]

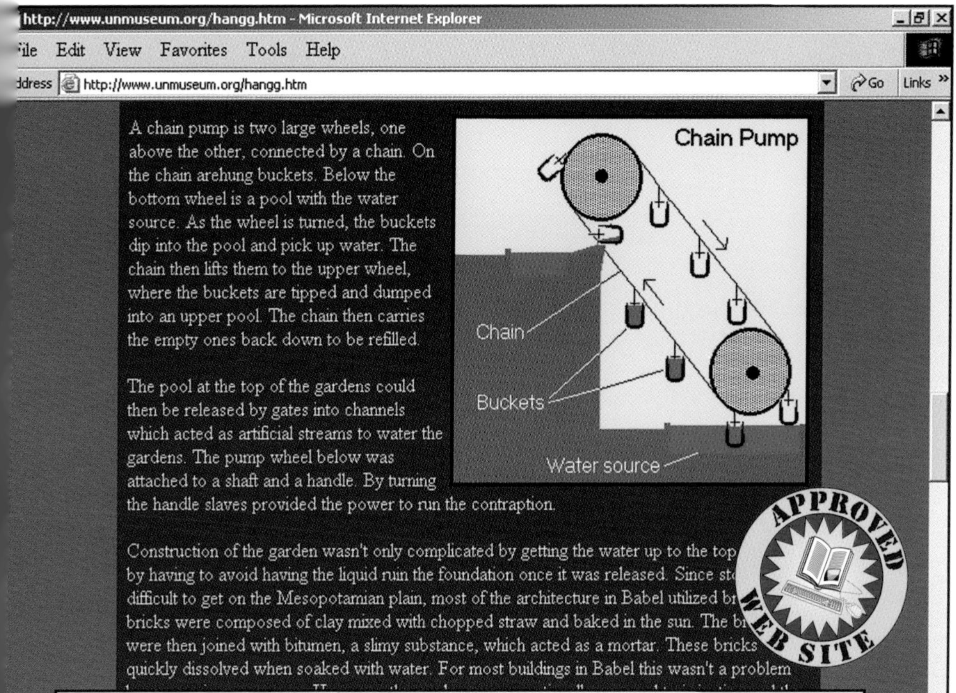

http://www.unmuseum.org/hangg.htm - Microsoft Internet Explorer

File Edit View Favorites Tools Help

Address http://www.unmuseum.org/hangg.htm Go Links

A chain pump is two large wheels, one above the other, connected by a chain. On the chain arehung buckets. Below the bottom wheel is a pool with the water source. As the wheel is turned, the buckets dip into the pool and pick up water. The chain then lifts them to the upper wheel, where the buckets are tipped and dumped into an upper pool. The chain then carries the empty ones back down to be refilled.

Chain Pump

Chain

Buckets

Water source

The pool at the top of the gardens could then be released by gates into channels which acted as artificial streams to water the gardens. The pump wheel below was attached to a shaft and a handle. By turning the handle slaves provided the power to run the contraption.

Construction of the garden wasn't only complicated by getting the water up to the top by having to avoid having the liquid ruin the foundation once it was released. Since st difficult to get on the Mesopotamian plain, most of the architecture in Babel utilized br bricks were composed of clay mixed with chopped straw and baked in the sun. The br were then joined with bitumen, a slimy substance, which acted as a mortar. These bricks quickly dissolved when soaked with water. For most buildings in Babel this wasn't a problem

APPROVED WEB SITE

Bringing water from the Euphrates River to irrigate the Hanging Gardens would have been a nearly-impossible task. It is likely that the ancient Babylonians used a chain pump to overcome this obstacle. This page is part of **The UnMuseum: The Hanging Gardens of Babylon** Web site.

A chain pump is set up as two large wheels, one on top of the other. The wheels are joined by a chain with buckets hung on various links of the chain. The water comes from a pool located below the bottom wheel. As the wheel is turned, the buckets dip into the pool and scoop up the water. The chain raises the buckets to the upper wheel, tipping and dumping the buckets into another pool of water. The chain then returns the empty bucket back down to be refilled again and again.[5]

The pool at the top of the gardens flowed downhill, watering the gardens as it did. The pump wheel was attached to a shaft and a handle below. By turning the handle, the constant muscle power of slaves provided the power to run the operation.[6]

The Seven Wonders of the World: The Hanging Gardens of Babylon

Access this Web site from http://www.myreportlinks.com

The Hanging Gardens of Babylon were supposedly built by King Nebuchadnezzar for his wife, Queen Amyitis. Read more about this amazing garden on this Web site.

EDITOR'S CHOICE

A Quest to Find the Gardens

The Hanging Gardens of Babylon may have endured in some form through to the time of Alexander the Great. Since 1899, archaeologists have worked to excavate the site where they believe the Hanging Gardens once existed.

German archaeologist Robert Koldewey discovered a basement with fourteen large rooms with stone arch ceilings while excavating the South Citadel (fortress that guarded the palace). According to ancient records, only two locations in the city had used stone during their construction. These were the north wall of the Northern Citadel and the Hanging Gardens. Koldewey had already found stone at the north wall of the Northern Citadel. This made it seem likely to Koldewey that he had found the cellar of the gardens in the South Citadel.[7]

As Koldewey continued to explore the site, he thought he found many of the features reported to have existed in the gardens. For example, a room with three large, strange holes in the floor was discovered. Koldewey concluded this must have been the site of the chain pumps that raised the water to the gardens' roof. Others believe that this was simply a storeroom used to keep food to feed the slaves.[8] Unfortunately, there is no conclusive proof that any of the structures Koldewey found were part of the structure of the Hanging Gardens.

If the gardens did exist, it took great architectural and engineering skills to create them, as well as the irrigation system that supplied the water. This is why the Hanging Gardens of Babylon are considered one of the seven wonders of the ancient world.

Chapter 4 ▶

Temple of Artemis at Ephesus

The Temple of Artemis was first built around 550 B.C. It was located in the Greek city of Ephesus, on the west coast of modern Turkey. It was one of the largest temples ever built by the ancient Greeks and was among the earliest temples to be built entirely of marble. This temple is often referred to as the Temple of Diana

▲ *The Temple of Artemis at Ephesus was built and rebuilt many times. The temple that is considered to be an ancient wonder was finished around 550 B.C. It was rebuilt sometime around 356 B.C. before it was torn down again over six hundred years later.*

The goddess Artemis in Greek mythology was known as the goddess Diana in Roman mythology. The people of Ephesus continued to worship Artemis well after other Greek gods were no longer worshipped. This statue of Ephesus is in the National Archaeological Museum of Naples in Italy. The image is part of an online resource called **Temple of Artemis.**

because Diana is the Roman name for the Greek goddess Artemis. She was the goddess of the hunt, the moon, fertility, and wild animals, among other things.

Building the Temple

The Temple of Artemis that is one of the seven wonders of the ancient world was not the first Temple of Artemis built at that location. There had first been a few small wooden temples built there. The first Temple of Artemis made of stone was built about 800 B.C., near the river at Ephesus. That temple was destroyed and later rebuilt over a period of several hundred years. It was reported that the earliest temple contained a sacred stone fallen from the planet Jupiter.[1]

A Lydian king by the name of Croesus conquered Ephesus in the 500s B.C. Although he destroyed much of the city, he spared the temple. Over time, he amassed great wealth. The local priests told him that he was becoming so wealthy that he was in danger of angering the gods. As a result, Croesus paid for the Temple of Artemis to be enlarged and expanded. This enlarged temple was designed by a Greek architect named Chersiphron and his son, Metagenes.[2] The scale of the work is evident from the story that when Chersiphron was faced with the challenge of raising the great entrance to the temple, he actually contemplated suicide.[3]

The temple's inner space consisted of a double row of at least 106 columns, each believed to be about 60 feet (18.29 meters) high.[4] The foundation was approximately 257 feet (78.5 meters) long by 430 feet (131 meters) wide.[5] The temple was adorned with bronze statues chiseled by such artists as Phidias, Polycleitus, Kresilas, and Phradmon.

The marble used for Croseus' temple was found seven miles (11.27 kilometers) away. Moving the 40-ton blocks was a major challenge.[6] Wagons could not support the weights of the blocks so Chersiphron devised a plan. He built a machine with two large wooden wheels on each end. He fit a 40-ton block between the two wheels. He connected them so that they could be pulled by oxen. As the wheels rolled, the oxen pulled the heavy blocks, which served as the axle for the wheels.

What Remains of the Temple Today

On July 21, 356 B.C., a man named Herostratus burned down the temple in order to get his name immortalized.[7] Coincidentally, that was also the same night that Alexander the Great, one of the greatest military leaders in history, was born. Legend is that Artemis was too busy assisting at the birth of Alexander and could

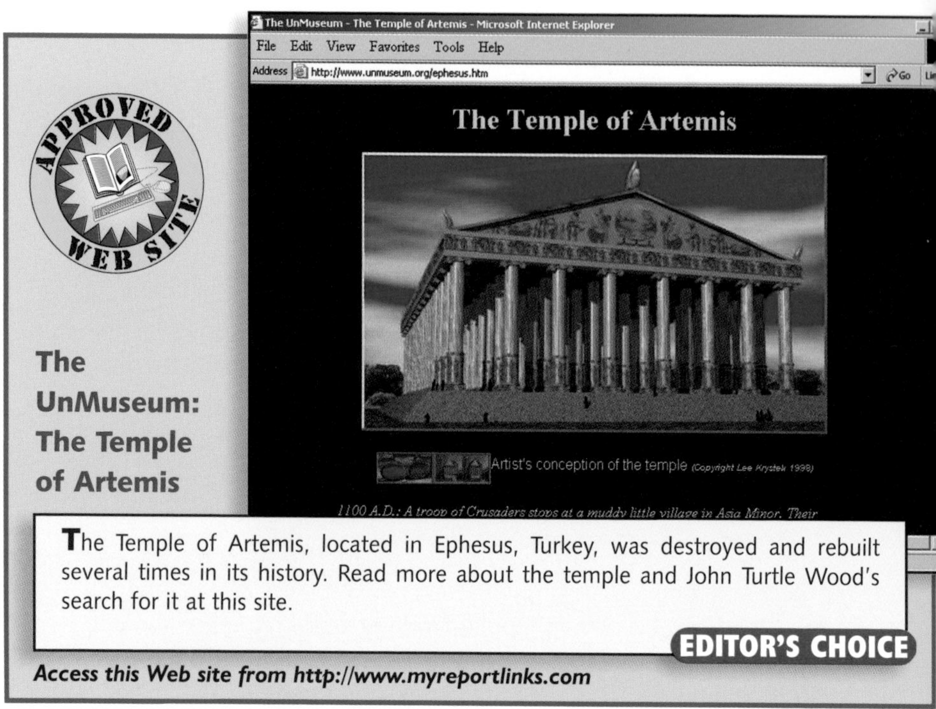

The UnMuseum: The Temple of Artemis

The Temple of Artemis, located in Ephesus, Turkey, was destroyed and rebuilt several times in its history. Read more about the temple and John Turtle Wood's search for it at this site.

EDITOR'S CHOICE

Access this Web site from http://www.myreportlinks.com

not save the temple. The Ephesians began rebuilding the temple almost immediately after it was burned.

The Temple of Artemis was the last of the great goddess temples to remain open. People worshipped their goddess there well after the beginning of Christianity. The rebuilt temple was burned by the Goths in A.D. 262. St. John Chrysostom, a well-known Christian preacher, had the entire structure torn down in A.D. 401.[8] All that survives is the excavated temple podium and one reconstructed column. The British Museum in London houses some of the second temple's sculptures as well.

Chapter 5 ▶

STATUE OF ZEUS

In ancient times the Greeks held an important festival called the Olympic Games. The Olympics were first held in 776 B.C. in honor of the king of their gods, Zeus. Athletes traveled from faraway lands to compete in the games. The Olympics were held every four years at a shrine to Zeus located on the west coast of Greece in a region called Peloponnesus. The games helped to unify the Greek city-states. A sacred truce was declared during the games, and wars were stopped. Safe passage was given to all traveling to the site, called Olympia, for the season of the Olympics.

Building of a Statue

By the fifth century B.C. the games had grown in importance, and a larger temple was needed. It was decided, however, that the temple alone was not worthy of the

An artist's rendition of the Statue of Zeus. The statue is said to have been so enormous that if the statue were able to stand up, it would go straight through the roof of the temple.

This is the original entrance to the Olympic Stadium. The Olympic Games became so popular that a larger, more impressive temple with the Statue of Zeus was needed nearby.

king of the gods. To fix this, a statue was to be designed in the image of Zeus and erected and housed in the large temple.

Phidias, a Greek sculptor, was picked to design the Statue of Zeus. He was well-respected for having made a 40-foot- (12-meter-) high statue of the goddess Athena for the Parthenon in Athens, another famous temple. However, the statue of Zeus would become his best-known work. Phidias crafted a 43-foot- (13-meter-) high statue of ivory and gold set on a marble base.[1]

The statue filled the western end of the temple. Phidias portrayed Zeus draped in a gold robe, wearing gold sandals, and seated on a throne. But the head of Zeus was near the roof of the temple. This amazed historians and poets of those times.

 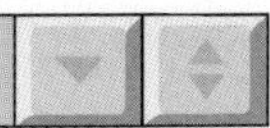

The statue of Zeus is so big that if he were to stand, he would go through the roof.

His whole massive body sat on a throne made of cedarwood and inlaid with ebony, ivory, gold, and jewels. His gold, sandaled feet rested on a large footstool. Below the footstool was a black marble basin used to collect olive oil that was poured over the statue to help prevent the ivory from cracking. Zeus' right hand held a winged victory figure symbolizing triumph in the Olympic Games. In his left hand he held his emblem, a shining scepter with an eagle perched on top. He wore an olive wreath around his head. Fine details of lilies and animals were carved into his clothing.[2]

What Remains of the Statue of Zeus Today

By the end of the A.D. 300s, Christianity had spread throughout much of Europe. The Christians banned the worship of Greek and Roman gods and all other pagans.[3] Greek gods and goddesses, such as Zeus and Athena, were not allowed to be worshipped. The sanctuary at Olympia was no longer used when Emperor Theodosius abolished the Olympic Games in A.D. 394. The games were later revived in 1896 to promote understanding and friendship among nations.

The statue of the Olympian Zeus still continued to awe onlookers. Because of its popularity, it was moved to the major city of Constantinople (now known as Istanbul, Turkey) for everyone to see. However, in A.D. 462, a fire damaged the city and destroyed the statue.

French archaeologists working on the Olympia site in 1829 were able to locate the outlines of the temple. They also found fragments of a sculpture showing the labors of the Greek hero Hercules.[4] These pieces were sent off to Paris where they are on display today at the Louvre, a famous art museum.

German archaeologists made an expedition to Olympia in 1875. Over five summers, they discovered more fragments of the

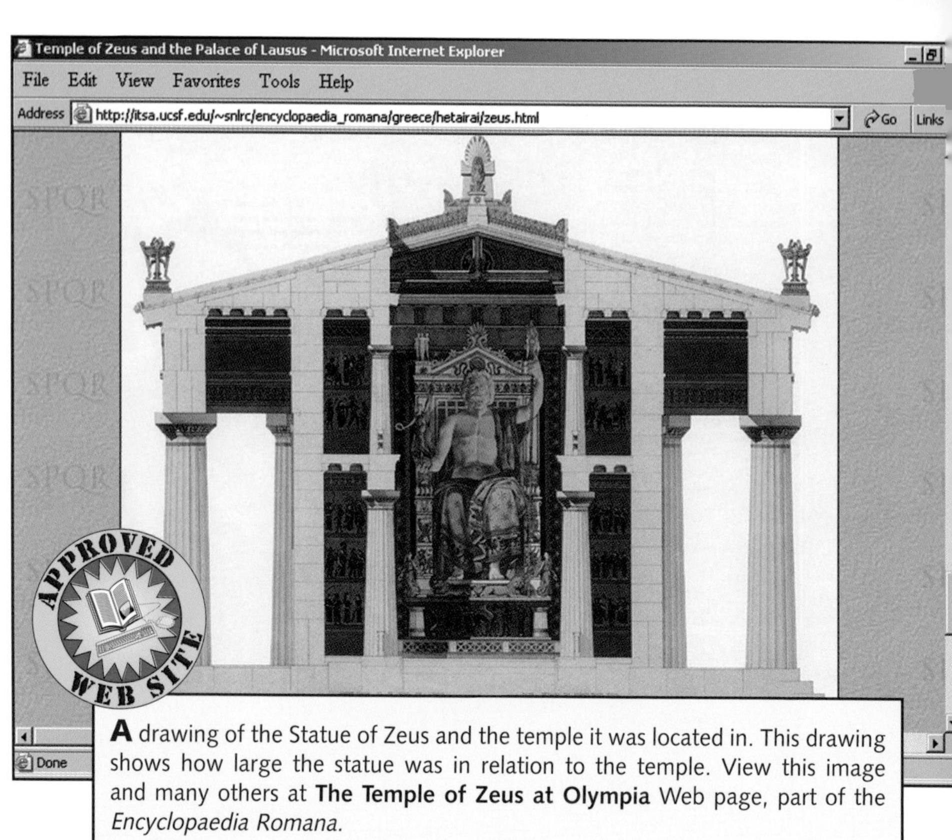

A drawing of the Statue of Zeus and the temple it was located in. This drawing shows how large the statue was in relation to the temple. View this image and many others at **The Temple of Zeus at Olympia** Web page, part of the *Encyclopaedia Romana*.

temple's sculptures, as well as the remains of a pool in the floor that contained the olive oil for the statue of Zeus.[5]

The workshop of Phidias was found during the course of another excavation that took place during the 1950s. It was unearthed below the foundation of an early Christian church.[6] Among the items found were a piece of an elephant's tusk that was used for its ivory, plaster, instruments used for sculpting, molds made of clay, and an area for shaping bronze.

The Olympic stadium has been restored at the site. Little is left of the temple except for a few columns. The statue, which was most likely the most magnificent work at Olympia is gone. But it will still keep its place on the list of wonders of the ancient world.

Chapter 6 ▶

MAUSOLEUM AT HALICARNASSUS

The Mausoleum at Halicarnassus was a large marble tomb built around 353 B.C. to hold the remains of King Mausolus of Caria. Mausolus was the ruler of the city of Halicarnassus and surrounding territories for twenty-four years.

The mausoleum was located in what is now Bodrum, on the Aegean Sea, in southwestern Turkey. This 135-foot- (41.15-meter-) high tomb was built by King Mausolus' grieving queen, Artemisia. In honor of this structure, the English word for all large tombs is *mausoleum.*[1]

Building the Mausoleum

Queen Artemisia employed five of the best sculptors of the Greek world to decorate her husband's mausoleum. They were Scopas, Bryaxis, Leochares, Timotheos, and Praxiteles.[2] The first four sculptors were each responsible for one side of the tomb. Praxiteles' job was to design a huge four-horse chariot on top of a twenty-four-step pyramid to be placed atop the tomb. The total height of the mausoleum with the statue on top was 148 feet (45 meters). The height of the pyramid rose to 22.3 feet (6.8 meters) and the chariot group standing atop measured 19.7 feet (6.0 meters).[3]

The foundation of the mausoleum was made with a green volcanic stone. On top of the foundation was a large podium. The podium had a height of 66 feet (20.2 meters). It was also made of green volcanic rock, but this rock was encased in marble. The green stone was found nearby. The marble and other stones used

This is artist Howard David Johnson's impression of how the Mausoleum at Halicarnassus may have looked. There are many differing opinions.

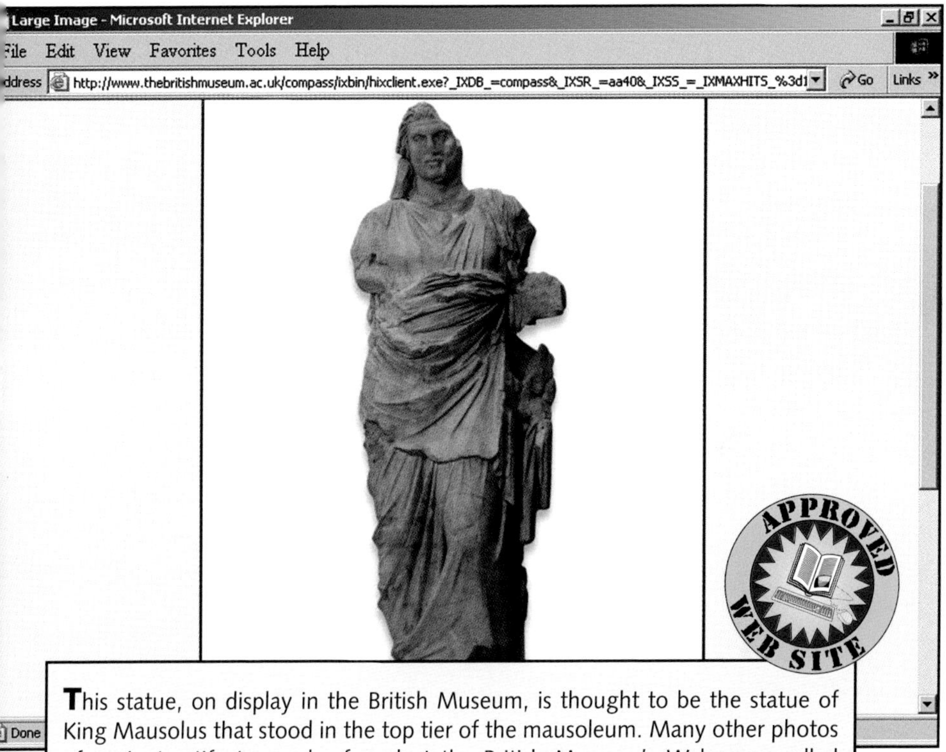

This statue, on display in the British Museum, is thought to be the statue of King Mausolus that stood in the top tier of the mausoleum. Many other photos of ancient artifacts can be found at the British Museum's Web page called **Mausoleum at Halikarnassos.**

EDITOR'S CHOICE

for building had to be brought in from far away. On top of the foundation was a structure called a cella, that consisted of thirty-six columns. The columns were each 29 feet (8.84 meters) high.

The mausoleum was decorated with two continuous sculptured borders called friezes. One showed battle scenes from the Greek war with the Amazons, as well as a chariot race. The other showed the mythological battle of the Lapiths against the centaurs, which were creatures with the upper body of a human and the lower body of a horse. There were also freestanding figures such as lions, life-size or larger, standing on a blue limestone base.

Soon after Mausolus died, Artemisia was challenged. Rhodes was an island in the Aegean Sea between Greece and Asia Minor that had been conquered by Mausolus. When the Rhodians heard

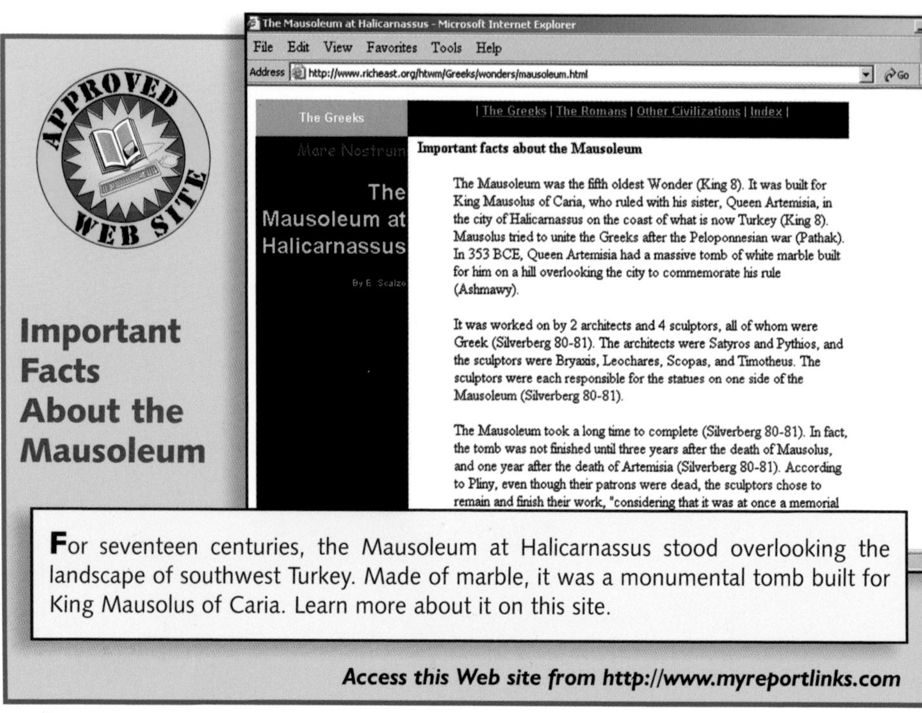

Important Facts About the Mausoleum

For seventeen centuries, the Mausoleum at Halicarnassus stood overlooking the landscape of southwest Turkey. Made of marble, it was a monumental tomb built for King Mausolus of Caria. Learn more about it on this site.

Access this Web site from http://www.myreportlinks.com

of his death, they rebelled by sending a fleet of ships to capture the city of Halicarnassus. They thought that now that Mausolus was dead, Halicarnassus would be easy to capture. Artemisia, knowing the fleet was on the way, was facing a crisis. She came up with a plan. She commanded her ships to sail to a secret location at the city's east end harbor. There, they would wait in hiding for the ships from Rhodes to anchor.

Artemisia's fleet then made a surprise attack after the Rhodian troops went ashore to invade. They captured the Rhodian fleet, towing it out to sea. Artemisia sent her own soldiers sailing back to Rhodes on the invading ships. When the people of Rhodes saw their ships returning, they thought they had been victorious. They were tricked when they found out the ships actually held Artemisia's soldiers. Rhodes was easily captured.[4]

What Remains of the Mausoleum Today

The mausoleum overlooked the city of Halicarnassus for about seventeen centuries. It survived when Alexander the Great conquered Halicarnassus in 334 B.C., and again during pirate attacks in 62 and 58 B.C. although it was slightly damaged.[5]

A series of earthquakes between A.D. 1000 and 1400 shattered the remaining columns and sent the chariot to a crash landing. By 1404 only the very base of the mausoleum was still recognizable. In 1494, crusaders known as the Knights of St. John of Malta, built an immense castle using blocks that they had taken from the rubble of the mausoleum. The lime mortar used to join the blocks was made out of burned marble from some of the mausoleum's statues and columns.

There have been many excavations done at the site of the mausoleum. Famous British archaeologist Sir Charles Newton excavated the site between 1856 and 1858. He discovered statues of lions that had adorned the mausoleum. He also found a broken stone chariot wheel, and two of the larger-than-life statues of Mausolus and Artemisia that stood at the pinnacle of the building.

From 1966 to 1977 there was a Danish excavation that discovered the remains of an offering of food for Mausolus. They found the remains of whole sheep, goats, oxen, doves, a goose, some chickens, and a large amount of eggs.

The remaining works of art from this wonder of the ancient world stand as an exhibit to its greatness in the Mausoleum Room at the British Museum.

Chapter 7

COLOSSUS OF RHODES

Built around 282 B.C., the Colossus of Rhodes was located in the harbor of the island of Rhodes. Rhodes is now part of the country of Greece. The island of Rhodes is located in the Mediterranean Sea below the southwestern tip of Asia Minor, where the Aegean Sea meets the Mediterranean Sea. There are no eyewitness accounts of the standing colossus to tell us what it looked like. No one has ever constructed a copy of the colossus, either. Much of what we do know about the colossus comes from the writings of ancient historians Pliny the Elder, Strabo, and Philo. They had

The Colossus of Rhodes was a statue of Helios, the patron god of the island of Rhodes. The colossus stood by the entrance to the harbor in much the same way that the Statue of Liberty stands in New York Harbor.

either passed along stories of others who had seen the colossus or had viewed the fallen remains of the statue.

The Colossus of Rhodes was a huge 108-foot (33-meter) bronze statue of the sun god, Helios, the patron god of Rhodes. The colossus was designed to pay tribute to Helios. The people believed Helios helped the city survive a siege by Demetrius Poliorcetes, the king of Macedonia, in 305 B.C.[1] Demetrius, also known as Demetrius the Besieger, withdrew from the island after meeting his match in Rhodes. He abandoned his siege engines (large machines—including catapults that threw 175-pound [80-kilogram] rocks). The Rhodians sold these weapons to pay for the building of the Colossus of Rhodes. A Greek sculptor by the name of Chares was hired to create this massive statue.

Today, the island of Rhodes is part of the country of Greece.

Assembling the Colossus of Rhodes

Glistening in the sun and towering over the buildings, the Colossus of Rhodes impressed both the people of Rhodes as well as foreign visitors. The statue, a symbol of unity for the people of Rhodes, took Chares more than twelve years to complete. Chares may have designed Helios wearing a wreath of flames and flowing hair that looked like it was blowing in the breeze. These were characteristics of the sun god as depicted on the coins of this time period.

A popular tale from the Middle Ages announced that the statue straddled the harbor mouth overlooking the water. However, it would have been virtually impossible to build the structure in that position. It is more likely that the statue stood upright, similar to the way the Statue of Liberty was erected.

Because the statue was going to be so large, Chares had to cast the figure in sections. He cast the feet first, setting them on a base made of white marble. Then, using carefully prepared and sculpted molds, the lower legs were cast upon the feet. And so Chares worked his way up, and the colossus grew with each section added. Supported internally by an iron framework of horizontal crossbars and weighted blocks of stone, colossus was a hollow structure.

As he worked upward, a hill of earth was continually raised, providing Chares with a platform to work from. Chares never saw what the statue looked like until he cast the very last part and the hill of earth was finally removed. As Chares could not truly see what he was working on until the colossus was completed, his feat is even more impressive. The English word *colossal* comes from the Colossus of Rhodes.

As Rhodes was a major trade center, supplies would have been easily imported. The amount of bronze needed to cast a statue of this size would have used up all of the island's reserve of copper and tin needed to make bronze.

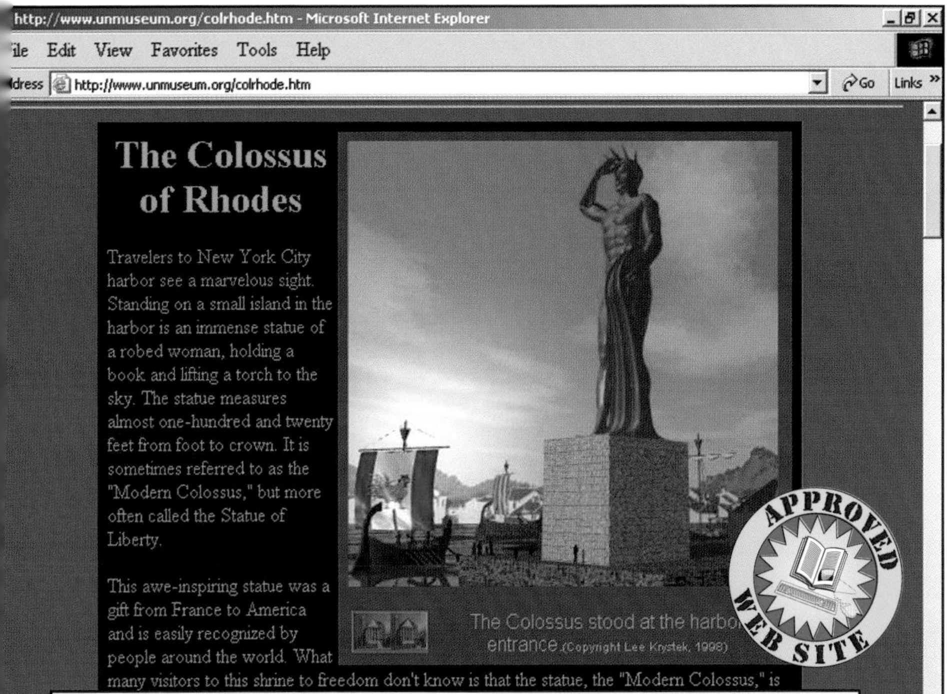

http://www.unmuseum.org/colrhode.htm - Microsoft Internet Explorer

File Edit View Favorites Tools Help

Address http://www.unmuseum.org/colrhode.htm Go Links

The Colossus of Rhodes

Travelers to New York City harbor see a marvelous sight. Standing on a small island in the harbor is an immense statue of a robed woman, holding a book and lifting a torch to the sky. The statue measures almost one-hundred and twenty feet from foot to crown. It is sometimes referred to as the "Modern Colossus," but more often called the Statue of Liberty.

This awe-inspiring statue was a gift from France to America and is easily recognized by people around the world. What many visitors to this shrine to freedom don't know is that the statue, the "Modern Colossus," is

The Colossus stood at the harbor entrance (Copyright Lee Krystek, 1998)

APPROVED WEB SITE

Read what an ancient Greek geographer and an ancient Greek historian had to say about the Colossus of Rhodes. This is another illustration of how the Colossus may have looked. It is included on the UnMuseum's **The Colossus of Rhodes** Web site.

What Remains of the Colossus Today

The Colossus of Rhodes stood for little more than fifty years until an earthquake in 224 B.C. toppled it. The city planned to rebuild it, but an oracle told the people of Rhodes not to do so or the city would face misfortune. A Syrian merchant carted away the metal ruins of the fallen colossus in A.D. 653. Prior to that, the colossus was left there as a tourist attraction.

Chapter 8

The Lighthouse (Pharos) of Alexandria

The Lighthouse of Alexandria was the first lighthouse in the world. At the time it was built it also had the distinction of being the world's second tallest building. (The Great Pyramid of Giza was the tallest.) The lighthouse was needed so that ships could be safely guided into the harbor of Alexandria, a bustling Egyptian city.

Construction of the lighthouse began during the rule of the Egyptian king, Ptolemy I. He became the ruler of Egypt after Alexander the Great died in 323 B.C. Ptolemy wanted to make sure the lighthouse would be impressive and signify that Alexandria was a growing and prosperous port city. This magnificent structure took fifteen years to build, and by the time it was finished Ptolemy was dead. His son, Ptolemy II, ascended to the throne. He was present at the dedication ceremony for the Pharos that took place in 283 B.C.

The Pharos of Alexandria looked much like a modern skyscraper. It was surrounded by statues of sphinxes and other fascinating sculptures of the time period.

This drawing of the Lighthouse of Alexandria shows the presumed structure of the Pharos. Archaeologists have found coins depicting the lighthouse, which is why we have a good idea of how it looked.

Building the Lighthouse

Architect Sostratus of Knidos was called upon to design and oversee the construction of the lighthouse. When it was finished, Sostratus was so proud of his work that he wanted to carve his name into the foundation. King Ptolemy II, though, refused this request. Instead, the king wanted his own name to be the only one on the building. Sostratus, however, was a clever man. Without anyone knowing, he chiseled the following message into the foundation: "*Sostratus, the son of Dexiphanes, the Cnidian, dedicated this to the Savior Gods, on behalf of those who sail the seas.*"[1]

He then covered this inscription with plaster and chiseled Ptolemy's name into the plaster. Plaster is a material that weakens over time, and as the years went by, the plaster chipped away. Ptolemy's name was eventually gone, and in its place was Sostratus' declaration.

The lighthouse was built on the island of Pharos off the coast of Alexandria. It was not long before the building was named after the island. Since then, the word *pharos* became a synonym for "lighthouse." Pharos became the root of the word lighthouse in the French, Italian, Spanish, and Romanian languages.[2]

The completed pharos was about 443 feet (135 meters) high.[3] The lighthouse did not look like the lighthouses that we see today. Instead, it looked more like a modern skyscraper. A person had to enter the lighthouse by going up a ramp that was built on one side of the tower. The building had three levels. To get to the upper levels, a large spiral ramp was built so that horse-drawn carriages could pull goods and materials up to the top sections.

The lowest tier was a barracks for the soldiers who guarded the lighthouse and the island. Their animals and supplies were kept in the lower tier as well. On top of the lowest section was an eight-sided tower. Above the tower was a portion of the building shaped like a cylinder. At the peak of the cylinder was the beacon chamber. This is where the Egyptians kept a fire burning that provided the light for the lighthouse at night. A large mirror was used to reflect the sun out to sea as a beam of light during the day. It has been said that this beam could be seen from 100 miles (160.93 kilometers) away.[4] The roof of the beacon chamber contained a large statue, which is thought to have been of either Zeus or Poseidon, the god of the sea.

The Remains of the Lighthouse

Other than the Pyramids of Giza, which are still standing, the Pharos of Alexandria was the last of the first six ancient wonders to be destroyed. It safely guided sailors into the city harbor for more than fifteen hundred years. Unfortunately, it was destroyed by two earthquakes. One shook the lighthouse in A.D. 1303 and the next in 1323. Remains and rubble of the ruined pharos stayed there until around the year 1480. Then, a medieval fort was built on the site by the Egyptian sultan Qaitbay.[5]

A team of scuba divers went to examine the site in the fall of 1994. They were searching the bottom of the harbor for artifacts that may have been from the pharos. They found large blocks of stone and used underwater measuring devices to create a map of the seafloor. They plan to examine the area further.

Underwater archaeological investigation of Pharos - Microsoft Internet Explorer

File Edit View Favorites Tools Help

Address http://www.unesco.org/csi/pub/source/alex6.htm

Figure 2. Site of the Pharos of Alexandria: raising a fragmentary sphinx with no inscriptions. Photo: Stéphane Compoint/Sygma.

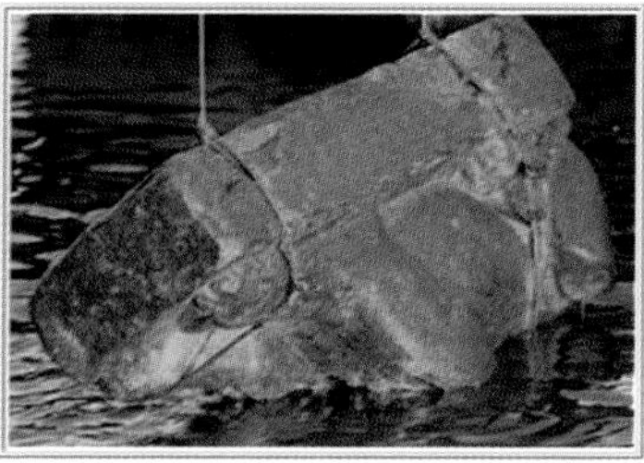

Several sculptures belong to the pharaonic era; there were 28 sphinxes, bearing the insignia of the Pharaohs Sesostris III (XII dynasty), Sethi I, Ramses II (XIX dynasty) and Psammetic II (XXVI dynasty) (Fig. 2). Their dates th... from the Middle Kingdom up to the last dynasties, or the mid-19th century BC to the early-6th century BC.

The presence of some pharaonic elements cannot fail to surprise us. Fortunately, two egyptologists fr... Corteggiani and Georges Soukiassian, were team members; underwater, they deciphered the hierogly... monuments bear. Several facts must be pointed out immediately: each sphinx is different from every oth... the possibility that they formed part of an approach to a monument. All the inscriptions describe scenes o... divinities of Heliopolis, as do the inscriptions on the obelisks found at the underwater site. In the Hellenistic era, ... venerable sanctu... nd

APPROVED WEB SITE

The excavation of the bottom of the sea around where the Lighthouse of Alexandria once stood is an ongoing project. Teams of divers have been finding pieces of the lighthouse's foundations and the statues that once stood around it. **The Underwater Archaeological Investigations of the Ancient Pharos** Web site is where to find this image and many others.

Other divers have located a large number of Egyptian statues in the place of where the pharos once stood. They have found that huge statues of Ptolemy II and his queen stood outside the lighthouse. These statues are even older than the lighthouse. It is believed that these statues were brought from other locations to adorn the front of the lighthouse.

It will be exciting in the years to come to see what other scientific discoveries will be made as more excavations of the seven wonders of the ancient world take place. Maybe one day we will be able to find out exactly how ancient people were able to create such magnificent buildings and monuments without a modern world's advancements in technology.

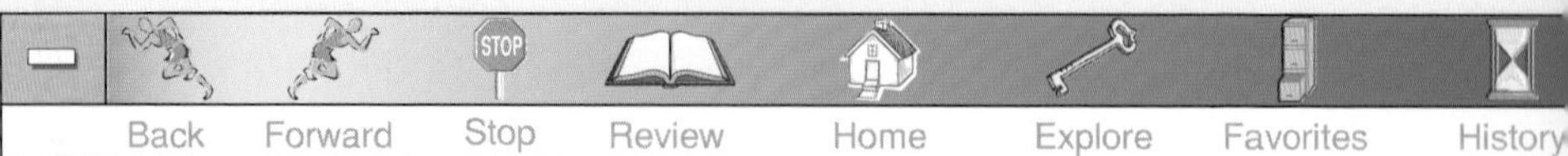

Report Links

The Internet sites described below can be accessed at
http://www.myreportlinks.com

The Seven Wonders of the Ancient World
Editor's Choice An overview of each of these ancient monuments and temples.

Destinations: The Seven Wonders of the Ancient World
Editor's Choice Take a virtual tour of the ancient wonders.

Nova Online: Pyramids
Editor's Choice Explore the pyramids of Giza.

The UnMuseum: The Temple of Artemis
Editor's Choice The most famous shrine to the fertility goddess.

The Seven Wonders of the World: The Hanging Gardens of Babylon
Editor's Choice The world's most famous gardens are profiled at Cleveleys Web site.

Mausoleum at Halikarnassos
Editor's Choice View the British Museum's collection of mausoleum artifacts.

The Colossus of Rhodes
A site with many images of paintings of the Colossus.

Egypt: Secrets of the Ancient World
Explore the pyramids of Egypt with *National Geographic.*

The Great Pharos Lighthouse
Learn about the great Pharos of Alexandria.

The Hanging Gardens of Babylon
The mythology and history of the Hanging Gardens of Babylon.

Helios
Information about the Greek sun god.

Hillman Wonders of the World: Colossus of Rhodes
The Colossus of Rhodes Web page from Hillman Publications.

Historic Figures: King Khufu (2609–2584 B.C.)
Learn more about the builder of the Great Pyramid.

Important Facts About the Mausoleum
A brief overview of the Mausoleum at Halicarnassus.

Lighthouse of Alexandria
Interesting facts about the Lighthouse of Alexandria.

Report Links

The Internet sites described below can be accessed at http://www.myreportlinks.com

Nebuchadnezzar
Nebuchadnezzar was the king of Babylon who built the Hanging Gardens.

Phidias' Workshop
Phidias created the Statue of Zeus in the workshop discussed at this Web site.

The Private Lives of the Pyramid-Builders
Learn about the ancient Egyptians who built the pyramids.

Ptolemy I Soter, The First King of Ancient Egypt's Ptolemaic Dynasty
The king of Egypt who had the Lighthouse of Alexandria built.

Pyramids of Giza
View images of ancient Egyptian tombs.

Statue of Zeus at Olympia
Historical facts on the Statue of Zeus.

Temple of Artemis
Ancient historian Pliny's account of the Temple of Artemis.

The Temple of Artemis at Ephesus
Brief history of the Temple of Artemis.

The Temple of Zeus at Olympia
Read excerpts from primary documents describing the Statue of Zeus.

Underwater Archaeological Investigations of the Ancient Pharos
Join an expedition trying to find out more about the Pharos of Alexandria.

Underwater Ruins off Alexandria
Excavating the waters surrounding Pharos Island.

The UnMuseum: The Colossus of Rhodes
The Colossus of Rhodes was the inspiration for the Statue of Liberty.

The UnMuseum: The Hanging Gardens of Babylon
A historian's view of the Hanging Gardens of Babylon.

Welcome to the Tour of Olympia!
Olympia is the home to the Statue of Zeus.

Who was Mausolus?
Read about the famous king of Caria for whom the mausoleum was built.

Asia Minor—Peninsula of land between the Black Sea and the Aegean Sea, with the Mediterranean Sea to the south. Most of this land is part of Turkey.

channel—A passage that a stream of water runs through.

Crusaders—Christian soldiers who fought to take the holy land back from the Muslims. These battles took place in the eleventh, twelfth, and thirteenth centuries.

crypt—A room that is located partially or entirely underground.

excavate—To dig a hole or to reveal the surface of an object by digging away a covering.

frieze—A decorative horizontal band.

ionic—The second oldest of the three types of classical Greek architecture; characterized by elaborate details.

irrigation—A man-made system designed to water lands that usually receive little rainfall or moisture.

mausoleum—A large tomb built above ground.

Media—An ancient land that was located in what is now northwestern Iran. The Medes were conquered by Cyrus the Great in 550 B.C.

mortar—Building material mixture that is used to bind together bricks and stones.

oracle—A person believed to have the power to receive and pass on messages from the gods.

pagan—Relating to a religion that is based on nature.

substructure—The part of a structure, such as the foundation, that supports the rest of the structure.

superstructure—The part of a structure that is constructed above the foundation.

temple—A building used for religious worship.

terrace—One of a series of horizontal ridges built on a slope.

Chapter Notes

Chapter 1. Seven Wonders of the Ancient World

1. There are many conflicting figures for the measurements of the seven wonders of the ancient world. To maintain consistency, we have used the measurements listed in *Time Almanac 2003,* as well as *The Seventy Wonders of the Ancient World,* edited by Chris Scarre.

Chapter 2. Pyramids of Giza

1. Chris Scarre, ed., *The Seventy Wonders of the Ancient World* (London: Thames & Hudson, 2002) pp. 21–22.
2. Paul Jordan, *The Seven Wonders of the Ancient World* (London: Longman/Pearson Education, 2002), p. 134.
3. Dr. Ian Shaw, "Building the Great Pyramid," October 28, 2002, <http://www.bbc.co.uk/history/ancient/egyptians/great_pyramid_print.html> (March 19, 2005).
4. Ibid.
5. Scarre, p. 24.
6. Shaw, "Building the Great Pyramid."
7. Scarre, p. 25.
8. Ibid.
9. Allen Winston, "The Pyramid of Khufu at Giza in Egypt, The Pyramid Proper, Part II: Internal and Substructure, n.d.," <http://www.touregypt.net/featurestories/greatpyramid3.htm> (March 21, 2005).
10. Ibid., p. 26.

Chapter 3. The Hanging Gardens of Babylon

1. Lee Krystek, "The Hanging Gardens of Babylon," 1998, <http://www.unmuseum.org/hangg.htm> (October 28, 2004).
2. Cleveleys Web site, "The Seven Wonders of the World: The Hanging Gardens of Babylon," <http://www.cleveleys.co.uk/wonders/gardensofbabylon.htm> (July 14, 2004).
3. Krystek, "The Hanging Gardens of Babylon."
4. Ibid.
5. Ibid.
6. Ibid.
7. Cleveleys Web site, "The Seven Wonders of the World: The Hanging Gardens of Babylon."
8. Paul Jordan, *The Seven Wonders of the Ancient World* (London: Longman/Pearson Education, 2002), p. 116.

Chapter 4. Temple of Artemis at Ephesus

1. SevenWondersWorld, "Seven Wonders of the World—Temple of Artemis," n.d. <http://www.sevenwondersworld.com/wonders_of_world_artemis_temple.html> (July 14, 2004).
2. Ibid.
3. Paul Jordan, *The Seven Wonders of the Ancient World* (London: Longman/Pearson Education, 2002), pp. 96–97.

4. “The Temple of Artemis (Diana) at Ephesus,” Destinations, 1997, <http://www.cnn.com/TRAVEL/DESTINATIONS/9705/seven.wonders/artemis.html> (March 15, 2004).

5. Ibid.

6. Chris Scarre, ed., *The Seventy Wonders of the Ancient World* (London: Thames & Hudson, 2002), p. 32.

7. SevenWondersWorld, “Seven Wonders of the World—Temple of Artemis.”

8. Ibid.

Chapter 5. Statue of Zeus

1. Chris Scarre, ed., *The Seventy Wonders of the Ancient World* (London: Thames & Hudson, 2002), pp. 33–34.

2. Ibid., p. 34.

3. Ibid., p. 36.

4. Cleveleys Web site “The Seven Wonders of the World: The Statue of Zeus at Olympia,” n.d., <http://www.cleveleys.co.uk/wonders/statueofzeus.htm> (July 14, 2004).

5. Ibid.

6. Ibid.

Chapter 6. Mausoleum at Halicarnassus

1. “The Mausoleum at Halicarnassus,” Destinations, 1997, <http://www.cnn.com/TRAVEL/DESTINATIONS/9705/seven.wonders/mausoleum.html> (March 15, 2004).

2. Chris Scarre, ed., *The Seventy Wonders of the Ancient World* (London: Thames & Hudson, 2002), p. 38.

3. Ibid., p. 39.

4. “The Seven Wonders of the World: The Mausoleum of Halicarnassus,” n.d., <http://www.cleveleys.co.uk/wonders/maussoleum.htm> (July 14, 2004).

5. Ibid.

Chapter 7. Colossus of Rhodes

1. Chris Scarre, ed., *The Seventy Wonders of the Ancient World* (London: Thames & Hudson, 2002), p. 42.

Chapter 8. The Lighthouse (Pharos) of Alexandria

1. Paul Jordan, *The Seven Wonders of the Ancient World* (London: Longman/Pearson Education, 2002), p. 42.

2. Lee Krystek, “The Pharos Lighthouse,” n.d. <http://www.unmuseum.org/pharos.htm> (November 15, 2003).

3. Chris Scarre, ed., *The Seventy Wonders of the Ancient World* (London: Thames & Hudson, 2002), p. 47.

4. Krystek, “The Pharos Lighthouse.”

5. Edgar J. Banks, *The Seven Wonders of the Ancient World* (New York: The Knickerbocker Press, 1916), p. 187.

Further Reading

Anderson, Dave. *The Story of the Olympics.* New York: W. Morrow, 2000.

Ash, Russell. *Great Wonders of the World.* New York: Dorling Kindersley, 2000.

Chrisp, Peter. *Alexander the Great: The Legend of a Warrior King.* New York: Dorling Kindersley, 2000.

Clayton, Peter, and Martin Price. *The Seven Wonders of the Ancient World.* London: Routledge, 1988.

Cox, Reg, and Neil Morris. *The Seven Wonders of the Ancient World.* Parsippany, N.J.: Silver Burdett Press, 1996.

Curlee, Lynn. *Seven Wonders of the Ancient World.* New York: Atheneum Books for Young Readers, 2002.

Hicks, Peter. *Ancient Greece.* Austin, Tex.: Raintree Steck-Vaughn, 2000.

Howe, Helen, and Robert Howe. *Ancient and Medieval Worlds.* White Plains, N.Y.: Longman, 1992.

Jackson, Kevin and Jonathan Stamp. *Building the Great Pyramid.* Buffalo, N.Y.: Firefly Books, 2003.

Kent, Peter. Great *Building Stories of the Past.* New York: Oxford University Press, 2001.

McLeish, Kenneth. *Seven Wonders of the World.* New York: Cambridge University Press, 1989.

McNeese, Tim. *The Pyramids of Giza.* San Diego, Calif.: Lucent Books, 1997.

Romer, John, and Elizabeth Romer. *The Seven Wonders of the World: A History of the Modern Imagination.* New York: Sterling Publishing, Co., 2001.

Scarre, Chris. *The Seventy Wonders of the Ancient World.* London: Thames & Hudson, 2002.

Index